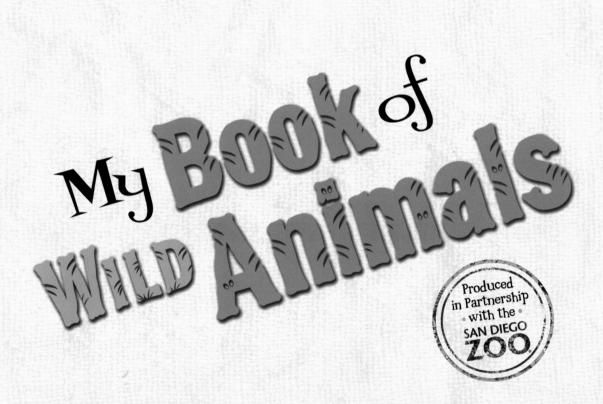

My Book of Wild Animals

Produced in Partnership with the SAN DIEGO ZOO

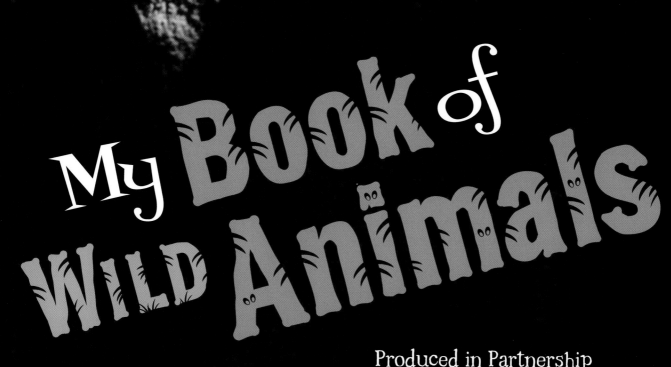

My Book of Wild Animals

Produced in Partnership
with the SAN DIEGO ZOO®

ideals children's books®
Nashville, Tennessee

ISBN-13: 978-0-8249-5561-8
ISBN-10: 0-8249-5561-7

Published by Ideals Children's Books
An imprint of Ideals Publications
A Guideposts Company
535 Metroplex Drive, Suite 250
Nashville, Tennessee 37211
www.idealsbooks.com

Color separations by Precision Color Graphics, Franklin, Wisconsin

Printed and bound in Mexico by RR Donnelley

Library of Congress Cataloging-in-Publication Data on file

10 9 8 7 6 5 4

Photographs: Creative Services, Zoological Society of San Diego

Designed by Eve DeGrie

Ideals Publications is a proud supporter of the San Diego Zoo and the San Diego Zoo's Wild Animal Park and will contribute 7% of the proceeds of each purchase of this item to support global conservation programs. The Zoological Society of San Diego is a California not-for-profit corporation located at 2920 Zoo Drive, San Diego, CA 92112. This purchase is not tax-deductible.

Wildbeasts™ is used by the San Diego Zoo® to promote worldwide conservation. Purchasing this product supports the San Diego Zoo's efforts to protect the survival of animals in captivity and those in the wild through research and education. The San Diego Zoo participates in international conservation projects in five geographical regions around the world.

We believe that even one endangered species is one too many. To learn more about Wildbeasts™, visit www.wildbeasts.org. To make a donation to the San Diego Zoo's conservation efforts, visit www.sandiegozoo.org.

Gorillas

Male gorilla

GORILLA STUFF

HEIGHT: males, 5.6 to 6 feet; females, up to 5 feet

WEIGHT: males, 300 to 500 pounds; females, 150 to 200 pounds

LIFE SPAN: about 35 years

NUMBER OF YOUNG AT BIRTH: usually 1, rarely 2

SIZE AT BIRTH: 4 to 5 pounds

CONSERVATION STATUS: endangered

Male gorilla

GENTLE GIANTS

Gorillas are the largest of all primates—the group of animals that includes monkeys, lemurs, orangutans, chimpanzees, and humans. Gorillas are peaceful, family-oriented, plant-eating animals.

KNUCKLE-WALKERS

Gorillas stand upright, but they prefer to walk using their hands as well as their legs. Their arms are much longer than their legs, and they can use the backs of their fingers like extra feet when they walk. Gorillas and chimpanzees are the only animals able to knuckle walk.

SEE-FOOD DIET

Almost everything a gorilla eats is plant material, so life in the forest is like living in a huge restaurant. Gorilla food includes leaves, stems, fruits, seeds, and roots. And gorillas love to eat— it's their favorite activity! An adult male will eat up to 40 pounds of food each day. Gorillas' large stomachs can hold the bulky food they eat. Strong jaws help them chew tough stems.

EVERY DAY IS MOVING DAY

A gorilla troop doesn't stay in the same place for more than a day. Each morning the silverback leads his troop to a new area where food is plentiful. After a morning of munching, adult gorillas gather leaves, twigs, and branches to make a day nest for resting while the youngsters play. After their nap, the gorillas will eat again until bedtime, when they make yet another nest, either on the ground or in a tree, for a good night's sleep. Gorillas never use the same nest twice.

Troop of gorillas

Hair This!
Gorillas are very hairy, but not on their faces, palms, and soles of their feet.

TROOP LEADER

A group of gorillas living together is called a troop. There can be 5 to 30 gorillas in a troop, led by a strong, experienced male known as a silverback. He is responsible for the safety and well being of the members of his troop. The silverback makes all the decisions, such as where the troop will travel for food each day, when they will stop to eat or rest, and where they will spend the night.

Sometimes a young male from another troop will challenge the silverback. The silverback will beat his chest with cupped hands, scream, bare his teeth, then charge forward. Sometimes he will break off branches and shake them at the intruder.

I Nose You!
No two gorilla noses are alike! Researchers in the wild take close-up photos of each gorilla's face to help identify individuals.

WHERE IN THE WORLD ARE GORILLAS?

RANGE: African continent, mainly along the equator

HABITAT: tropical rain forests, mountain slopes, and bamboo forests

Baby lowland gorilla

BABY BUSINESS

A female gorilla is ready to have babies of her own when she is about 8 years old. Her baby grows quickly. At 5 to 6 months old it learns to walk, and by 18 months of age it can follow mom on foot for short distances. The safest place for the youngster, however, is its mother's back.

Mother and 3-month-old baby

...ale Sumatran tiger, 8 feet long
HEAVIEST: male Siberian tiger, 400 pounds and up
LIFE SPAN: 15 to 20 years
NUMBER OF YOUNG AT BIRTH: 2 to 3, up to 7
SIZE AT BIRTH: 2.2 pounds
CONSERVATION STATUS: endangered

Sumatran tiger

Malayan tiger

BLACK AND WHITE AND ORANGE ALL OVER

Tigers are recognized by their orange, black, and white striped coat which is good camouflage in the long grass. Dark stripes on a pale background break up the tiger's outline as it lies in wait for prey to come near. Tigers can also be black with tan stripes, all white (albino), or white and tan. The "white tigers" found in some zoos are not albino, but rather the white-and-tan color variation with blue eyes. (True albinos have pink eyes.)

Bengal tiger

HUNTING GEAR

Tigers' front paws are large with 5 toes on each. The tiger pulls his claws inside while he walks, which keeps them sharp. Tigers mark their territory by scratching on trees. This also sharpens the claws.

Sumatran tiger

Bengal tiger

Malayan tiger

GO JUMP IN A LAKE

Some cats do like water—and tigers are among them. On a hot, steamy day in the Asian forest, tigers will take to the river to cool off. In colder climates, they enjoy the snow.

LOVIN' THOSE LEFTOVERS

Tigers like pigs and deer for dinner, while in some parts of Asia they may bring down a rhino or elephant calf. A tiger quietly stalks its prey for 20 or 30 minutes. Then it grabs its prey by the neck with large canine teeth and powerful jaws. A tiger kills once or twice a week. After it's stuffed itself, it covers the leftovers with grass and dirt. The tiger keeps coming back for the next few days for small snacks.

TIGER BABIES

Tiger cubs are born small and helpless, but the mother must leave them alone while she hunts. Tiger cubs don't hunt on their own until they are 2 years old.

No Fake I.D.s
Each tiger has its very own stripe pattern. Researchers who observe tigers can identify individuals by their unique stripes.

Siberian tiger

Tiger Talk	
CHUFFLE:	"Hello," or sometimes, "I'm so happy."
GRRRR:	"This is my territory" or a male calling a female
ROARRR:	"I'm warning you!"

WHERE IN THE WORLD ARE TIGERS?

RANGE: small pockets of Asia

HABITAT: tropical rain forests, snow-covered coniferous and deciduous forests, mangrove swamps, and drier forest areas

Alligators & Crocodiles

American alligator

Say Ahhhhh!
A croc's tongue can't move. It's attached to the bottom of its mouth.

African slender-snouted crocodile

African dwarf crocodile

IS IT AN ALLIGATOR OR A CROCODILE?

Alligators have wide, U-shaped, rounded snouts. Crocodiles have longer, more pointed, V-shaped snouts. Crocodiles live in saltwater habitats. Alligators live in freshwater habitats. If the fourth tooth on the lower jaw sticks up over the upper lip, it's a crocodile. Don't get too close looking for that tooth!

MOTHER LOVE—CROC STYLE

Crocs take care of their babies for the first year of their life. Some species make a mound nest out of soil and plants; others dig a hole in the sandy beach. Then mama croc lays her eggs and settles in to guard them from predators. When the babies start to hatch, they make grunting or barking noises from *inside the egg*. They use a tooth on the end of their snouts called an "egg tooth" to break out of the leathery eggshell. Some croc moms help by gently biting the egg to open it.

American alligator

Slender-snouted crocodile

That's a Croc!
All the species of alligators, caimans, crocodiles, and gharial together are known as "crocodilians" or "crocs."

COMING TO THEIR SENSES
Crocs hear through slits on their heads. When they dive into the water, the slits close up to keep water out. Crocs have eyes on top of their heads so they can see as they

Eye of a slender-snouted crocodile

cruise the water looking for food. They have good night vision because their vertical pupils open wider than round ones and let in more light. Crocs have taste buds to taste their food, and special organs in their snouts give them a great sense of smell.

American alligator

I HAVEN'T EATEN IN YEARS!
All crocs store fat in their tails. Some big adults can go without eating for as long as two years!

WHAT'S FOR DINNER?
Crocs are carnivores and eat whatever they can catch in the water or along the banks. They eat fish, turtles, frogs, birds, pigs, deer, buffalo, and monkeys, depending on the size of the croc.

COME ON IN, THE WATER'S FINE!
Crocs are most at home in or near the water. They look like logs floating in a swamp or washed up on shore. Crocs can hold their breath underwater for more than an hour.

African slender-snouted crocodile

CROCODILE TEARS
Crocs "cry," but the only purpose of the tears is to get rid of excess salt in the croc's body.

WHERE IN THE WORLD ARE CROCS?

ALLIGATOR AND CAIMAN

RANGE: alligators, southern United States and eastern China; caimans, Central and South America

HABITAT: grassy swamps and slow-moving rivers

CROCODILE

RANGE: Mexico, Central and South America, Africa, Southeast Asia, and Australia

HABITAT: grassy swamps and slow-moving rivers

Polar Bears

POLAR BEAR STUFF

SHOULDER HEIGHT: up to 5.3 feet
LENGTH: 6.6 to 10 feet
WEIGHT: males, 660 to 1,760 pounds; females, 330 to 660 pounds
LIFE SPAN: 25 to 30 years
NUMBER OF YOUNG AT BIRTH: 1 to 4, 2 average
SIZE AT BIRTH: 1.3 pounds
CONSERVATION STATUS: vulnerable

FROZEN FOOD

Polar bears are mainly meat eaters, and their favorite food is seal. They will also eat walrus, caribou, beached whales, grass, and seaweed. Polar bears are patient hunters, staying motionless for hours above a seal's breathing hole in the ice, just waiting for dinner to pop up.

BUTTON UP YOUR OVERCOAT

Polar bears look white, but their hair is really clear, hollow tubes filled with air. These long hairs stick together when wet and form a waterproof barrier that keeps the thick, furry undercoat dry.

WHERE IN THE WORLD ARE POLAR BEARS?

RANGE: along the coasts and inland streams and lakes of Alaska, Canada, Greenland, Norway, and Russia

HABITAT: arctic, tundra, and wooded habitats

WE'RE HAVING A HEAT WAVE

Polar bears are built to stay so warm in their cold habitat that sometimes they overheat and have to cool off in the icy water.

Mother and cub

Mother and cub

DEN MOTHER

A mother polar bear digs a den in the snow about the size of a telephone booth. Usually 2 cubs are born in December or January. The cubs are about the size of a rat, hairless, and blind. By April they weigh more than 20 pounds and begin to explore outside the den. When they are 2 years old, they are ready to be on their own.

NAP TIME

Polar bears do not hibernate when the temperature drops, but their bodily functions slow down. Many scientists call this "winter sleep," because the bears can easily be awakened. A mother polar bear can give birth and nurse her young during winter sleep.

Nose on Legs
The polar bear can smell a seal on the ice 20 miles away, sniff out a seal's den covered with snow, and find a seal's air hole in the ice up to a mile away.

BABY, IT'S COLD OUTSIDE!

Polar bears have blubber 2 to 4 inches thick that insulates the bears from the freezing air and cold water. Blubber is also a nutritional reserve when food can't be found. And it helps the bears float in the water, sort of like an inner tube.

Elephants

AFRICAN ELEPHANT STUFF

SHOULDER HEIGHT: males, 10.5 feet to 13 feet; females, 8.2 feet

WEIGHT: males, up to 15,000 pounds; females, up to 8,000 pounds

LIFE SPAN: more than 50 years

NUMBER OF YOUNG AT BIRTH: 1

WEIGHT AT BIRTH: 117 to 330 pounds, average 232 pounds

HEIGHT AT BIRTH: 26 to 42 inches

CONSERVATION STATUS: African forest elephant, endangered

WHERE IN THE WORLD ARE AFRICAN ELEPHANTS?

RANGE: Kenya, Zimbabwe, Tanzania, Zambia, Uganda, Democratic Republic of the Congo, Namibia, and national parks in South Africa

HABITAT: grassland savanna and open woodland

African elephant

Drink 480 Glasses of Water a Day
Elephants drink about 30 gallons of water EVERY day.

African or Asian?
There are 2 different kinds of elephants: African and Asian. Can you tell them apart?

African Elephants	Asian Elephants
• have large ears shaped like the continent of Africa	• have smaller ears
• both males and females have visible tusks	• only the males have visible tusks
• their skin is very wrinkly	• their skin is not as wrinkled
• their backs are swayed	• their backs are dome-shaped.
• the end of their trunk works as if they have 2 fingers there to help them pick things up.	• they only have 1 "finger" at the end of their trunks

Asian elephant

ASIAN ELEPHANT STUFF

SHOULDER HEIGHT: 8.2 to 9.8 feet
WEIGHT: males average 11,000 pounds (5.5 tons); females average 6,000 pounds (3 tons)
LIFE SPAN: more than 50 years
NUMBER OF YOUNG AT BIRTH: 1
WEIGHT AT BIRTH: 110 to 250 pounds
CONSERVATION STATUS: endangered

Bigger Than Dumbo
The largest elephant on record was an adult male African elephant. It weighed about 24,000 pounds (12 tons) and was 13 feet tall at the shoulder!

OH MAMA!
Both African and Asian elephants live in herds made up of related females, called cows, and their offspring. The leader of the herd is the matriarch, usually the oldest and most experienced female. The matriarch decides when and where the herd will eat, rest, and travel.

PLACES TO GO, THINGS TO DO
Adult males, called bulls, don't live in a herd. Once male elephants become teenagers, they leave the herd. Only after they become adults will they visit other herds, and that is only for short periods of time to breed. Bulls do not take part in caring for the young.

WHERE IN THE WORLD ARE ASIAN ELEPHANTS?

RANGE: India, Nepal, and Southeast Asia

HABITAT: scrub forest and rain forest edge

African elephant herd

Orangutans

Female orangutan

DAYDREAMERS

Orangutans are the loners and the daydreamers of the great apes. While chimps and gorillas are usually found in groups called troops, orangutans are more solitary. Other apes might go from tree to tree searching for fruit, but an orang will just sit in the forest canopy for hours on end until the location of the hidden fruit seems to mysteriously reveal itself. Then it will swing over for its meal. Orangs have even been known to watch villagers use boats to cross the local waterways, and then untie a boat and ride it across the river on their own.

RELAXED PROBLEM SOLVERS

Scientists like to explain the orangutan's unique approach to problem solving with this example: If a chimp is given an oddly shaped peg and several different holes to try to put it in, the chimp will immediately try shoving the peg in various holes until it finds the hole that the peg fits in. But an orang will stare off into space, or even scratch itself with the peg. Then, after a while, it will offhandedly stick the peg into the correct hole while looking at something else that has caught its interest.

RANGE: northern Sumatra and parts of Borneo

HABITAT: rain forest

All Arms
An orangutan's arms stretch out longer than their bodies—over 7 feet from fingertip to fingertip!

Male orangutan

CHEEK TO CHEEK
When they are about 15 years old, male orangs develop large cheek pads. Female orangs find these pads very attractive. When males are fighting, they charge at each other and break branches. And if that doesn't scare one of them away, they grab and bite each other on the cheek pads or ears until one of them gives up and runs away.

TREE HOUSE
Orangutans spend most of their lives in trees and travel by swinging from branch to branch with their long arms. They usually build a new nest every night, but occasionally reuse one. They use leafy branches to shelter themselves from rain and sun and even drape large leaves over themselves like a poncho.

Mother and baby

8-month-old orangutan

IT'S YOU AND ME, MOM
Orangutans have the longest childhood of the great apes. Young orangs usually stay with their mothers until they're about 8 years old or older. The solitary animals must learn all the lessons of finding fruit, building night nests, and other survival techniques before they set off on their own.

males, up to 3,000 pounds; females, up to 14 feet
1,500 pounds
LIFE SPAN: 15 to 20 years
NUMBER OF YOUNG AT BIRTH: usually 1
SIZE AT BIRTH: 6 feet tall, 100 to 150 pounds
CONSERVATION STATUS: lower risk

DROPPING IN

When a giraffe baby, called a calf, is born, it drops to the ground head first, about a 6-foot drop. The fall and the landing don't hurt the calf, but they do cause it to take a big breath. The calf can stand up and walk after about an hour. Sometimes the mother will leave the calf alone for most of the day. The youngster sits quietly by itself until she returns.

Masai giraffe

A LOT OF HEART

A giraffe's heart is 2 feet long and weighs about 25 pounds. Giraffe lungs can hold 12 gallons of air.

Masai giraffe

LONG TONGUE

A giraffe's tongue is 18 to 20 inches long and blue-black. The color may keep the tongue from getting sunburned.

Young Masai giraffe

What Did You Say?
Giraffes can moo, hiss, roar, and whistle.

STAND UP STRAIGHT

A giraffe has 7 vertabrae in its neck, the same number as humans. Each giraffe vertebra is over 10 inches long. A giraffe's 6-foot neck weighs about 600 pounds!

WHERE IN THE WORLD ARE GIRAFFES?

RANGE: pockets of Africa, south of the Sahara Desert

HABITAT: savanna

Uganda/Baringo giraffe

Masai giraffe

HELLO, UP THERE!

Giraffes are the tallest land animals. Their legs are 6 feet long. The back legs look shorter than the front legs, but they are about the same length.

LUMPY HEAD

Both male and female giraffes have 2 distinct, hair-covered horns called *ossicones*. Male giraffes use their horns to playfully fight with one another. As male giraffes age, calcium deposits form on their skulls and other horn-like bumps develop.

Uganda/Baringo giraffe

EATING THE TREES

A giraffe can eat up to 75 pounds of leaves each day. They spend most of their day eating because they get just a few leaves in each bite.

Masai giraffe

CHEW IT AGAIN AND AGAIN!

The giraffe is a ruminant and has a stomach with 4 compartments that digests the leaves it eats. When giraffes aren't eating, they are chewing their cud. After they swallow the leaves the first time, a ball of leaves will travel all the way back up the throat into the mouth for more grinding.

PACE YOURSELF

When giraffes walk or run, both the front and back legs on one side move forward together, then the other 2 legs on the other side move forward. This is called "pacing."

TAIL

The giraffe has the longest tail of any land mammal. Tails can be 8 feet long, including the tuft on the end.

Flamingos

THE MORE THE MERRIER

Flamingos are social birds that live in groups of a few pairs to thousands or even tens of thousands. In East Africa, more than 1 million flamingos may gather together, forming the largest flocks of birds known.

THINK PINK AND ORANGE

The flamingos' pink or reddish color comes from the rich sources of carotenoid pigments (like the pigments in carrots) in the algae and small crustaceans that they eat. The Caribbean flamingos are the brightest, showing their true colors of red, pink, or orange on their legs, bills, and bodies.

UP, UP, AND AWAY

In order to fly, flamingos must run to gather speed, usually into the wind. In flight, flamingos stretch out their long necks and long legs. Their wings show black and red (or pink) coloration. When flying, flamingos flap their wings rapidly and almost continuously. They usually fly in large flocks and follow each other closely, taking advantage of the wind.

WHERE IN THE WORLD ARE FLAMINGOS?

RANGE: Africa, Asia, the Americas, and Europe

HABITAT: large, shallow lakes or lagoons

Adult flamingo sitting on nest

HOME IS IN THE MUD

A flamingo nest is just a mound of mud, about 12 inches high. The nest needs to be high enough to protect the egg from flooding and from the occasional intense heat at ground level. Both the male and female build the nest by pulling mud toward them with their bills. Flamingos lay a single large egg, which is kept warm by both parents. At hatching, a flamingo chick has gray down. It also has a straight, pink bill and pink legs, both of which turn black within a week.

Rest Awhile
Standing on one leg is the flamingo's most comfortable resting position.

A Place of Their Own
When the young birds leave the nest, they herd together in large groups, called creches.

FOOD FOR THOUGHT

The flamingo's bill is held upside down in the water. The flamingo feeds by sucking water and mud in at the front of its bill and then pumping it out again at the sides, trapping shrimp and other small water creatures in the flamingo's mouth.

Adult feeding chick crop milk

GOT MILK?

After hatching, the chick stays in the nest for 5 to 12 days. During this time, the chick is fed crop milk that comes from the parents' upper digestive tract. The mother, the father, and other flamingos feed the chick. The begging calls from the hungry chick stimulates the secretion of the milk.

Tortoises & Turtles

Leopard tortoise

TORTOISES & TURTLES

All turtles, tortoises, and terrapins are reptiles. They all have scales, lay eggs, and are ectothermic (cold blooded).

WHERE IN THE WORLD ARE TORTOISES & TURTLES?

RANGE: temperate and tropical regions except Antarctica

HABITAT: aquatic species: oceans, swamps, freshwater lakes, ponds, and streams; terrestrial species: deserts, forests, and grasslands

Stripe-necked turtle

Painted terrapin

AT THE DAY SPA
Some turtles groom each other. One turtle uses its jaws to pull algae and loose pieces of shell off the other. Then they switch places and the other grooms the first.

Roti Island snake-naked turtle

TERRAPIN

Terrapins can live on land, but always beside rivers, ponds, and lakes. Terrapins are often found in swampy areas. The word terrapin comes from a Native American word meaning "little turtle."

Painted terrapin

HOUSE ON LEGS

A turtle's shell is part of its skeleton. The turtle cannot crawl out of it, because the shell is permanently attached to the spine and the rib cage.

TORTOISES

Tortoises live on land and eat low-growing shrubs, grasses, and even cactus. Their feet are round and stumpy. Tortoises that live in hot, dry habitats use their strong legs to dig burrows. When it's too hot in the sun, they go into the cooler underground.

TURTLES

Turtles spend most of their lives in the water and most have webbed feet for swimming. Sea turtles are especially adapted for water, with flippers and a streamlined body shape. Other turtles live in freshwater, like ponds and lakes. They swim, but they also climb onto banks, logs, or rocks to bask in the sun.

Indochinese box turtle

WHAT'S FOR DINNER?

Most turtles and tortoises eat both plants and fish, snails, worms, or insects. Others eat only grasses, leafy plants, flowers, fruits, and even cactus. Some are specialists: the leatherback sea turtle and the hawksbill turtle dine on jellyfish, even poisonous ones. Other turtles have broad, expanded jaws for crushing the shells of mollusks.

What's the Difference?
The common names of turtle, tortoise, and terrapin usually refer to differences in where the species live.

Galápagos tortoise

Lions

Asiatic lion

LION STUFF

LENGTH: males, 5.6 to 8.3 feet; females, 4.6 to 5.7 feet
TAIL LENGTH: 27 to 41 inches
SHOULDER HEIGHT: males, 4 feet; females, 3.5 feet
WEIGHT: males, 330 to 550 pounds; females, 265 to 400 pounds
LIFE SPAN: 15 years in the wild
NUMBER OF YOUNG AT BIRTH: 1 to 6, usually 3 to 4
SIZE AT BIRTH: 3 pounds
CONSERVATION STATUS: Asian lion, vulnerable

LIVING WITH PRIDE

Lions are the only cats who live in large, social groups, called "prides." A pride is made up of 3 to 30 lions and consists of lionesses (mothers, sisters, and cousins) and their cubs, along with a few unrelated adult males. The pride has a close bond and is not likely to accept a stranger. The unrelated males stay a few months or a few years, but the older lionesses stay together for life. In dry areas with less food, prides are smaller, with 2 lionesses in charge. In habitats with more food and water, prides can have 4 to 6 adult lionesses.

NOT ALL CATS ARE ALIKE

Female Transvaal lion

Lions are the only members of the cat family to have males and females that look distinctly different. Only lions have a tuft of dark hairs on the tips of their tails, which helps them communicate with other lions in their pride.

Super Bowl Hero
A lion chasing down prey can run the length of a football field in 6 SECONDS.

WHERE IN THE WORLD ARE LIONS?

RANGE: parts of Africa and India's Gir Forest

HABITAT: grassy plains, savannas, open woodlands, and scrub country

ALL FOR YAWN AND YAWN FOR ALL

Lion researchers have noticed that some activities are "contagious" in prides. One lion will yawn, or groom itself, or roar, setting off a wave of yawning, grooming, or roaring!

Male Transvaal lion

Female and male Transvaal lion

KING OF THE BEASTS

Male lions eat more than the lionesses but bring in far less food (they hunt less than 10 percent of the time). But the males patrol, mark, and guard the pride's territory. Males also baby-sit with the cubs while the lionesses are out hunting. When new males try to join a pride, they have to fight the males already there. The lion's thick mane protects his neck against raking claws during fights.

Juvenile Transvaal lions

AN EATING MACHINE

Lions digest their food so quickly they can eat a second helping shortly after gorging themselves on dinner. They hunt antelope and hoofed animals, baby elephants or rhinos, rodents, reptiles, insects, crocodiles, and even buffalo and giraffes. Lions will steal prey from leopards, cheetahs, hyenas, or wild dogs. They will even eat prey that has spoiled.

JUST LION AROUND

A lion's life is filled with sleeping, napping, and resting. Over the course of 24 hours, lions have short bursts of intense activity, followed by long bouts of lying around that total up to 21 hours! Lions are good climbers and often rest in trees, perhaps to catch a cool breeze or to get away from flies. Researchers have often noticed lions lying around in crazy poses, on their backs with their feet in the air or legs spread wide open.

YOU GO, GIRLS!

Lions live in a matriarchal society. The lionesses work together to hunt and rear the cubs. During hunting, smaller females chase the prey toward the larger and heavier lionesses who ambush the prey.

Male Transvaal lion

Mandrills

MANDRILL STUFF

LENGTH: male, about 32 inches; female, about 22 inches
TAIL LENGTH: 2 to 3 inches
WEIGHT: male, average 55 pounds; female, 25 pounds
LIFE SPAN: up to 40 years
NUMBER OF YOUNG AT BIRTH: usually 1, sometimes 2
WEIGHT AT BIRTH: 1 to 2 pounds
CONSERVATION STATUS: endangered

Male mandrill

BIG AND BRILLIANT

Mandrills are one of the largest species of monkey in the world. Their furry head crests, manes, and beards are quite impressive, but what will really gets attention is their bright color. They have thick ridges along their noses that are purple and blue, their noses and lips are red, and their beards are golden.

WHERE IN THE WORLD ARE MANDRILLS?

RANGE: equatorial region of western Africa

HABITAT: primarily rain forest

LET'S DO TAKE-OUT

Mandrills have large cheek pouches inside their mouths that they stuff full of food to eat at a safer location. Mandrills spend most of their time on the ground, foraging for seeds, nuts, fruits, and small animals.

Mother and baby

Grin and Bare It

Mandrills shake their heads and "grin" widely to show their canine teeth, which can be over 2 inches long. This is a friendly gesture among mandrills.

OH BABY, BABY

Female mandrills usually give birth to 1 baby. The infant is born with a dark fur coat and can cling to its mother's belly immediately. At 2 months of age it starts to lose its baby hair and its adult coat comes in.

FAMILY LIFE

Mandrills live in troops of about 20. The dominant male is the leader and has the boldest, brightest colors. Super troops of several hundred mandrills may gather when food is readily available. The troop sleeps in a different tree each night.

Female mandrill

Male mandrill

Bald Eagles

BALD EAGLE STUFF

BODY LENGTH: 29 to 42 inches
WINGSPAN: 5.5 to 8 feet
WEIGHT: males, 6 to 9 pounds; females, 10 to 15 pounds
LIFE SPAN: 25 to 40 years
NUMBER OF EGGS: 1 to 3
CONSERVATION STATUS: threatened in southern Canada and most of the United States; abundant in its northern range, especially Alaska

ARE BALD EAGLES REALLY BALD?
Bald eagles' heads are covered with short white feathers. They are sometimes called American eagles, fishing eagles, Washington eagles, or white-headed eagles.

OUR NATIONAL SYMBOL
To symbolize the United States, the founders chose the bald eagle, a bird of prey found only in North America. Benjamin Franklin thought it was a poor choice because it sometimes steals food from other birds. He recommended the wild turkey.

WHERE'S THE WHITE HEAD?
Upon hatching, baby eaglets are fluffy and light gray. Just prior to leaving the nest, at about 12 weeks old, the youngsters' feathers turn dark brown. The distinctive white head and neck feathers won't appear until maturity.

Speed Freak
A bald eagle can reach a speed of up to 200 miles per hour when diving through the air to grab a meal.

GONE FISHIN'

Bald eagles have spiny scales and sharp talons on their toes for gripping slippery fish and keen eyes to see one. A hungry eagle perches on a tree above the water until it spies a fish near the surface. Then it swoops down and plucks the fish out of the water. The eagle flies back to its nest and, with its powerful, hooked beak, rips into its food.

EAGLE EYE

Bald eagles can see 4 to 7 times better than humans. They are able to see things sharply from quite far away. This, of course, helps them spot their next meal from high in the sky, or from a lofty perch in a tree or on a cliff ledge. Unlike our eyes, an eagle's eyes cannot move from side to side. To look around, the eagle turns its whole head.

FALLING FOR EACH OTHER

It is believed that bald eagles choose a mate for life. To impress each other, a male and female perform a dance in the sky. They lock on to each other's talons and tumble and twist in the air. At the last second they let go, just before reaching the ground.

HOME, SWEET NEST

The bald eagle is a master nest builder. A pair of eagles build their large nest high in a sturdy tree or sometimes on the ground if no tree is around. Year after year, they return to the same nest and add twigs, grass, moss, feathers, and branches to the original nest until it becomes huge. Sometimes a nest gets so heavy that its supporting branches break, and the nest comes crashing down.

Balancing Act

When a bald eagle loses a feather on one wing, it will lose a matching one on the other. This way it stays balanced.

WHERE IN THE WORLD ARE BALD EAGLES?

RANGE: Canada, United States, and northwest Mexico

HABITAT: coastlines, lakes, rivers, swamps, and marshes

Zebras

SEEING STRIPES

Each zebra has a unique stripe pattern. When zebras are huddled together, their stripes make it hard for a lion to pick out 1 zebra to chase. Different zebra species have different types of stripes, from narrow to wide. When stripes are painted on a wall, a zebra will stand next to them.

Hartmann's mountain zebra

All in the Family

Zebras live in family groups made up of a stallion, several mares, and their offspring.

LAWN MOWERS

Zebras eat grass and leaves and stems of bushes. Their strong front teeth clip off the tips and their back teeth crush and grind the food. Chewing wears the zebra's teeth down, but their teeth continue to grow.

WHERE IN THE WORLD ARE ZEBRAS?

RANGE: eastern and southern Africa

HABITAT: grasslands and savannas

GET YOUR KICKS

Zebras have excellent hearing and eyesight and can run at speeds of up to 35 miles per hour. Their powerful kicks can injure a lion. The stallion stays at the back of the group to defend against predators, while the mares and foals run from danger.

RUN, ZEBRA, RUN!

Zebra foals are dark brown and white at birth. They can run 1 hour after birth. The mare must remain with the group and cannot leave the foal. It must be up and running quickly in order to stay with its mother.

Damara zebra

SCRATCH MY BACK AND I'LL SCRATCH YOURS

When zebras stand head to back, apparently biting each other, they are actually nibbling on each other to pull out loose hair and give each other a good scratch.

SPLISH, SPLASH, OH, WHAT A BATH

Zebras take dust or mud baths. They shake the dirt off to get rid of loose hair and flaky skin. What's left protects them from sun, wind, and insects.

Hartmann's mountain zebra

Say Cheese!
Zebras have their own smile, a bared-teeth grimace that is a greeting and helps prevent aggression.

Damara zebra

Damara zebra

BETTER CLOSE YOUR MOUTH!

Zebras communicate with loud braying, barking, and soft snorting or *whuffling*. The position of their ears, how wide open their eyes are, and whether their mouths are open or their teeth bared all mean something to other zebras.

Kangaroos & Wallabies

Eastern red kangaroo

THE BIG GUYS

The red kangaroo, found most often on the open plains of inland Australia, can live on very little water. Maroon with a white face and belly, males are often referred to as "red flyers." Red kangaroos can be over 6 feet tall and weigh up to 200 pounds. When spooked, red kangaroos can leap across the outback in 10-foot-high, 39-foot-long bounds.

MYSTERIOUS MAMMAL MOVEMENT

When the kangaroo hops, both feet push off the ground at the same time. The larger kangaroos can cover over 15 feet per hop when cruising at top speed and have been clocked at more than 30 miles per hour in short bursts.

Western gray kangaroo

Southern yellow-footed wallaby

HAVE LEGS, WILL HOP

Kangaroos, wallaroos, and wallabies have back legs and feet that are much larger and more powerful than their front legs. Their tails are long, muscular, and thick at the base; the tail helps the animal balance and turn during hopping and provides support when the animal rests.

Troop of gray kangaroos

Mob Scene
A group of kangaroos is called a mob, a troop, or a herd. They are very social animals.

WHERE IN THE WORLD ARE KANGAROOS & WALLABIES?

RANGE: Australia and New Guinea

HABITAT: found in every habitat in Australia and in wet forests in New Guinea

New South Wales wallaroo

WHAT'S THE DIFFERENCE?

What's the difference between kangaroos, wallaroos, and wallabies? The main difference between a kangaroo and all the others is size. The 6 largest species are referred to as kangaroos.

New South Wales wallaroos

Parma wallabies

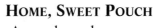
Play It Forward
Kangaroos cannot walk backwards.

HOME, SWEET POUCH

A newborn kangaroo is tiny and underdeveloped. The doe carries the newborn in a special pouch, called a *marsupium*, on her body. The joey stays in the pouch for several months, just drinking mother's milk. Joeys often peek their heads out of the pouch to have a look around weeks before they head out on their own.

Boas

Annulated boa

PUTTING THE SQUEEZE ON DINNER

Boas are *constrictors*. They grab their prey with their teeth, coil their bodies around the prey, and squeeze and squeeze. They squeeze so tight so that the prey animal cannot breathe and it suffocates. The snake then unhinges its jaw and swallows the prey whole, usually headfirst.

JUST HANGIN' AROUND

Boas that live in a dry environment usually hang out in rock crevices or in underground burrows made by other animals. The ones that live in forests blend into the leaves on the ground to stay hidden. All in all, a boa would rather avoid people than go looking for trouble.

YOU'RE ON YOUR OWN, KIDS

Boas give birth to live young. When baby boas are born, they are surrounded by a protective membrane. Mom goes on her way while the babies break out of the membrane. This makes the babies so hungry that they then go look for something to eat.

South American boa constrictor babies

It's the Truth!
Female anacondas grow much larger than the males.

Green anaconda

"WALK" A STRAIGHT LINE

Boas move by traveling forward in a straight line, which is known as "rectilinear progression." They stiffen their ribs to provide support, then lift the scales on their belly, move the scales forward so the loose ends grip the surface, and pushes the snake ahead. This type of movement works on the ground as well as in trees, and boas can even climb smooth surfaces. They are slow though, moving only about 1 mile per hour.

Emerald tree boa

Madagascar ground boa

Black-headed python

LOOKING FOR A HOT MEAL

Boas eat rodents, birds, lizards, frogs, and small to medium-sized mammals like opossums, monkeys, pigs, or deer. Boas are ambush hunters. They hide, then they lie still until one of those tasty animals comes walking by. The boa quickly strikes to catch it. *Yum, yum.*

WHERE IN THE WORLD ARE BOAS?

RANGE: Western North America, Central and South America, Africa, Madagascar, western Asia, and Pacific Islands

HABITAT: rain forests, swamps, woodlands, grasslands, savannas, and semidesert scrub lands

Solomon Island boa

WHAT'S THAT SMELL?

Boas "smell" by flicking their tongues in and out. This way of "smelling" helps them find their dinner. Most boas also have special temperature-sensitive scales around their mouths that can sense the heat of a nearby animal.

Macaws

MACAW STUFF

HEAVIEST: hyacinth macaw, 3 to 3.7 pounds
LIGHTEST: red-shouldered macaw, 4.5 to 5.9 ounces
LIFE SPAN: up to 50 years
NUMBER OF EGGS: 1 to 4, depending on species
CONSERVATION STATUS: Spix's macaw extinct in the wild; indigo macaw, critical risk; blue-throated macaw, red-fronted macaw, and hyacinth macaw, endangered

Hyacinth macaw

SCREECH, SQUEAL, AND SQUAWK

Screaming is a natural behavior for macaws. They do it to make contact with one another, to define territory, and sometimes just for fun. Loud screeching and squawking voices help make their presence known in dense rain forests. They can also imitate sounds and words that they hear, often practicing to themselves until they get it right.

Zooming Around

Macaws have a streamlined body and wings that don't flap deeply. The red-fronted macaw can fly at up to 40 miles per hour.

THE FAMILY THAT FLOCKS TOGETHER

Macaws live in pairs, family groups, or flocks of 10 to 30. Before dawn, the flock awakens, preens their feathers, and calls to one another. They fly to the day's feeding grounds—a grove of trees with ripe fruit. They feast until midday, when they settle down for a rest. In the afternoon they eat again until close to dusk.

Scarlet macaw

MUSICAL CHAIRS

At dusk, flocks of macaws return to their roosting site, where they call to each other to figure out who sits where. The sitting arrangement can change from day to day. Sometimes squabbles break out, but macaws rarely physically injure each other. Once everyone is settled, they quiet down, fluff out their feathers, and prepare to snooze through the night.

A SPLASH OF COLOR

The macaws' brightly colored feathers blend in with the green leaves, red and yellow fruits, and bluish shadows of the rain forest. Most macaws start out with gray or black eyes when they're young, which change to brown or yellow when they mature.

Red-fronted macaw

Blue and gold macaw

Blue and yellow macaw

TEST EVERYTHING

Macaws are intelligent and curious birds. They use their strong, agile toes to grasp things, and they like to play with interesting objects they find. They will examine the objects from different angles, move them with their feet, test them with their tongues, and toss them around.

BEAKS THAT BREAK

Macaws have large, strong, curved beaks designed to crush nuts and seeds. A macaw's beak is so strong it can easily crush a whole Brazil nut—or a person's knuckle.

MAY I SEE THE MENU?

Macaws eat a variety of ripe and unripe fruits, nuts and seeds, flowers, leaves, stems, insects and snails. Some species specialize in eating the hard fruits and nuts of palm trees.

Boney Tongue
A macaw's tongue is dry, slightly scaly, and has a bone inside it.

Hyacinth macaw

WHERE IN THE WORLD ARE MACAWS?

RANGE: Mexico and Central and South America

HABITAT: rain forest, forests along rivers, and grasslands with trees

Koalas

Just Hangin' Around

Koalas are slow-moving animals that sleep a lot and live in eucalyptus trees. They chew leaves and nap all day.

Is It a Koala Bear?

Koalas have round, fuzzy ears and look like a teddy bear. But koalas are not bears. They are members of a group of pouched animals called marsupials. Koala fur feels like the wool on a sheep.

Where in the World Are Koalas?

Range: southeastern and eastern Australia

Habitat: scrubland eucalyptus forest

Mother and joey

BABY IN THE POCKET
A newborn koala is called a "joey." It is the size of a jellybean, has no fur, and cannot see or hear. Soon after the joey is born, it crawls into its mother's pouch. It will stay there for the next 6 months. When the joey outgrows the pouch, it will ride on its mother's back. After about a year, it can live alone in the trees.

NOSING AROUND
When a joey learns to eat eucalyptus leaves, it goes after them with its mouth. Its nose gets in the way and pushes the leaves out of reach. Eventually it figures out how to grab leaves with its front paws and put them in its mouth.

Dirt for Dessert
Koalas eat a little dirt now and then to help them digest their eucalyptus leaf meal.

BORN TO CLIMB
A koala has claws on its hands and feet. It has 2 thumbs on each hand and strong arm and shoulder muscles. Koalas can leap from treetop to treetop.

EUCALYPTUS AGAIN?
Koalas only eat eucalyptus leaves. There are more than 600 different kinds of eucalyptus trees, but koalas prefer the leaves of about 3 dozen varieties.

Leopards

LEOPARD STUFF

LENGTH: 3 to 6 feet

TAIL: 23 to 44 inches

WEIGHT: males, 80 to 200 pounds; females, 62 to 132 pounds

LIFE SPAN: 12 to 15 years in the wild

NUMBER OF YOUNG AT BIRTH: 1 to 6, but usually 2 to 3 in a litter

SIZE AT BIRTH: 1 pound

CONSERVATION STATUS: all 8 subspecies, endangered

North Chinese leopard

SUPERCAT!

Leopards are strong swimmers, can run in bursts up to 36 miles an hour, leap 20 feet forward in a single bound, jump 10 feet straight up in the air, and climb 50 feet up a tree while holding a dead animal in its mouth, even one larger and heavier than itself.

SEEING SPOTS

Leopards have spots on their backs called rosettes. White spots on the tips of their tails and backs of their ears help leopards locate and communicate with each other in tall grass. Nearly black leopards live in the thick rain forests of Southeast Asia. They may look solid black, but they have a black-on-black rosette-patterned coat.

Persian leopard rosettes

Persian leopard

Indochinese leopard

Snow leopard

Clouded leopard

North Chinese leopard

A MIDNIGHT SNACK

Leopards hunt at night, and they use their vision and keen hearing. They stalk and pounce, grabbing their prey by the throat. Leopards are carnivores and will eat any meat they can get: monkeys, baboons, rodents, reptiles, amphibians, large birds, fish, antelope, cheetah cubs, and porcupines.

WHEN IS A LEOPARD NOT A LEOPARD?

Although both snow leopards and clouded leopards have "leopard" in their common names, they are different enough from the true leopards to have their own classifications within the cat family.

STALK, POUNCE, AND CHASE

Have you ever seen a housecat creep slowly after a bird or mouse? That's *stalking*. A quick leap and a grab with the claws is a *pounce,* and the *chase* begins if the prey gets away. Leopard cubs play stalk, pounce, and chase with their brothers, sisters, and even their mother. This is how they learn to hunt for food.

WHERE IN THE WORLD ARE LEOPARDS?

RANGE: Africa and Asia

HABITAT: forests, mountains, grasslands, and deserts

No Thanks, I'm Not Thirsty
The Persian leopard can live without ever drinking water. It gets the moisture it needs from food.

Giant Pandas

GIANT PANDA STUFF

LENGTH: about 5 feet (1.5 meters)
HEIGHT AT SHOULDER: 27 to 32 inches
WEIGHT: 220 to 330 pounds
LIFE SPAN: about 14 to 20 years
NUMBER OF YOUNG AT BIRTH: 1 or 2
SIZE AT BIRTH: about 4 ounces
CONSERVATION STATUS: endangered

WHAT HAPPENED TO DINNER?

When bamboo plants reach maturity, they flower and produce seeds, and the mature plant dies. All of the plants of a species growing in an area will bloom and die at the same time. When those plants die, pandas must move to another area to find another species of bamboo. As their habitat shrinks, pandas are often unable to move to another area.

BLACK AND WHITE AND LOVED ALL OVER

The giant panda is a national treasure in China and is protected by law. This unique bear has long been revered by the Chinese and can be found in Chinese art dating back thousands of years.

A Bachelor Life for Me
Pandas live alone except at breeding season.

Giant Panda Bears
The genetic code (DNA) in pandas' cells confirm that pandas are bears.

1½-year-old panda and mother

GYMNASTICS

Giant pandas are curious and playful, especially when they're young. They have unusually thick and heavy bones for their size, but they are very flexible and love to do somersaults.

Mother and 4½-month-old cub

EATING AGAIN?

Pandas live in cold and rainy bamboo forests high in the mountains of western China. They spend at least 12 hours a day eating. Because bamboo is so low in nutrients, pandas must eat as much as 84 pounds of it each day.

HOW TO EAT A BAMBOO STALK

A panda grasps the bamboo stalk with its 5 fingers and a special wristbone on 1 hand. The teeth peel off the tough outer layers of the bamboo stalk to get to the soft inner tissue. Now the panda bites down on the thick stalk with its strong jaw and chews. For an appetizer, the panda strips leaves off the bamboo stalks, wads them up, and swallows them whole. For a change, the giant panda occasionally eats grasses, bulbs, fruits, some insects, and even rodents.

WHERE IN THE WORLD ARE GIANT PANDAS?

Where, Oh Where, Is a Panda?
Today, only around 1,600 giant pandas survive in the wild.

RANGE: southwestern China, in 6 small forest fragments

HABITAT: damp, misty forests of bamboo and conifers, in altitudes above 4,000 feet

WHAT DID YOU SAY?

Pandas make a bleating sound similar to that of a lamb or goat kid. They also honk, huff, bark, or growl. Young cubs croak and squeal.

TINY GIANT

When born, giant pandas are about the size of a stick of butter. They have no fur and are completely helpless. The panda mother cares for her tiny cub. She cradles it in one paw and holds it close to her chest. For several days after birth, the mother does not leave the den, not even to eat or drink.

Mother and 4-month-old cub

Owls

OWL STUFF

LARGEST: Eurasian eagle-owl, over 2 feet

SMALLEST: elf owl, 5 to 6 inches

WEIGHT: typical owls, 1.5 ounces to 9 pounds; barn owls, 0.5 to 3 pounds

LIFE SPAN: 20 years or more

NUMBER OF EGGS: from 1 to 14 eggs; usually 2 to 6

CONSERVATION STATUS: 7 owl species at critical risk

Eurasian eagle-owl

American great grey owl

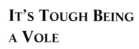

Spectacled owl

IT'S TOUGH BEING A VOLE

Owls compete with each other for territory and food, but fortunately owls of different species can coexist by hunting at different times of the day or night. The great gray owl, the ural owl, and the tawny owl all live in the same range, but the great gray owl is unique among owls in that it is a daytime hunter. It prefers voles as prey. The tawny owl also hunts voles, but only at night, and the ural owl hunts larger prey, such as squirrels.

WHERE IN THE WORLD ARE OWLS?

RANGE: every continent except Antarctica

HABITAT: virtually all, from the Arctic to the tropics

Barn owl

Shhh ... Mouse Alert
An owl can hear a mouse
stepping on a twig 75 feet away.
This is because they have 2 huge
ears that are incredibly sharp.

NIGHT VISION

Owls have eyes so big that they cannot move them. An owl must move its entire head to follow the movement of prey, but this gives the owl better focus, since both eyes are looking in the same direction. Although it seems that an owl can twist its head completely around, most owls actually turn their heads no more than 270 degrees in either direction.

BABY, IT'S COLD OUTSIDE

Owls live in the arctic, where the cold tundra is home to snowy owls. Thick, warm feathers cover even their bills and toes, providing effective insulation against roaring winds and freezing temperatures.

Western burrowing owl

NIGHT FLIGHT

Owls fly at night, and they fly low to the ground as they look for small rodents. Larger owls have been known to carry off young deer, weasels, and foxes.

Great horned owl

STEALTH BOMBER

Owls are silent in flight. Where other birds have stiff feathers that make a whooshing sound when they fly, owl feathers have soft edges that allow them to fly silently. This allows owls to swoop down on prey without being heard.

Lizards

IT'S ON THE TIP OF MY TONGUE!

The Madagascan chameleon has a sticky-tipped tongue which it can shoot out farther than the length of its body!

LIZARD ON YOUR FINGER

The smallest reptile in the world—dwarf gecko—can fit on the tip of your finger!

Green crested basilisk

Madagascar giant day gecko

WHAT IS A LIZARD?

In general, lizards have a small head, short neck, and long body and tail. And unlike snakes, most lizards have moveable eyelids. There are currently over 4,675 lizard species, including iguanas, chameleons, geckos, Gila monsters, monitors, and skinks.

WHERE IN THE WORLD ARE LIZARDS?

RANGE: southern Canada to the tip of South America, most of Europe and Asia, and all of Africa and Australia

HABITAT: all areas of the world except extreme cold and deep oceans

Sungazer

SLEEP ALL DAY, PLAY ALL NIGHT

Desert-dwelling lizards, like the ground gecko, usually sleep during the day under the warm sand, then come out when the sun has gone down.

OUCH, OUCH, OUCH!

To protect its feet from the hot sand, the sand lizard "dances" by lifting its legs up quickly, one at a time, or by resting its belly on the sand and lifting up all four legs at once!

San Diego horned lizard

Fijian iguanas

Something in Your Eye?
Most lizards have eyelids. But some lizards, like geckos, can't blink. They have a clear membrane that shields their eyes from dirt or bright sun.

Bamboo leaf-tailed gecko

DADDY NO-LEGS

Lizards that live in burrows have smaller legs than other lizards, or none at all. They can slither underground more easily than if they had long legs.

LIZARD HOMES

Some lizards live in trees. Tree dwellers have special toes and often a prehensile tail for grasping thin branches.

That's Fast!
The six-lined racerunner holds the record for the fastest speed reached by any reptile on land: 18 miles per hour.

Parson's chameleon catching worm

LOOKING FOR LUNCH

Most lizards eat insects, grabbing crickets, flies, grasshoppers, and more with long, sticky tongues or quick bites.

GLOSSARY

aggression: Hostile or violent behavior toward another.

albino: Animal that has no pigment in the skin and hair, which is white, and eyes, which are pink.

ambush: A surprise attack on something.

arctic: Relating to the regions around the north pole.

bamboo: A giant woody grass.

blubber: The fat of sea animals, especially whales and seals.

camouflage: An animal's natural coloring that allows it to blend in with its surroundings.

carnivore: An animal that eats meat.

carotenoid: Yellow, orange, or red color in plants.

classification: The arrangement of plants and animals in groups.

conifer: A tree with cones and evergreen needles.

constrictor: A snake that kills by coiling around its prey and squeezing it so it cannot breathe.

contagious: Something that can spread from one animal to another.

crèche: A nursery where babies are cared for.

crest: A comb or tuft of feathers.

critical risk: At a point of crisis.

crop: A pouch in a bird's esophagus where food is stored and prepared for digestion.

deciduous: A tree that sheds its leaves every year.

digest: To break down food in the stomach so the body can use it.

egg tooth: A hard white tooth that is used by an embryo bird or reptile for breaking out of an egg, which is later lost.

endanger: Putting something at risk.

environment: The surroundings in which a plant, animal, or person lives.

equator: An imaginary line around the earth equal distance from the poles.

eucalyptus tree: A fast-growing evergreen Australasian tree.

flock: A number of birds of one kind.

foal: A young horse or related animal.

forage: Search for food.

genetic code (DNA): Relating to genes or heredity.

gharial: A large fish-eating crocodile.

habitat: The natural home of an animal of an animal, plant, or other organism.

hibernate: A plant or animal spending the winter in a dormant state.

imitate: Take or follow as a model.

joey: A young kangaroo, wallaby, koala, or possum.

lagoon: A stretch of saltwater separated from the sea by a long sandbank or coral atoll.

mane: A growth of long hair on the neck of a horse, lion, or other animal.

mangrove: A tree that grows in muddy, coastal swamps.

mare: The female of a horse or other equine animals.

marsh: Area of low-lying land typically waterlogged at all times.

marsupial: Mammals that are born incompletely developed and carried in a pouch on the mother's belly.

matriarch: A female which is the head of a family or group.

membrane: A thin, pliable skin.

mollusk: Invertebrates with soft, unsegmented bodies.

nutrient: A substance that provides nourishment essential for growth.

pacing: When a four-legged mammal runs by lifting both legs on the same side together.

pigment: The natural coloring matter of plant or animal.

prehensile tail: Capable of grasping.

prey: An animal that is hunted and killed for food.

pride: A group of lions.

primate: Mammals that have hands, handlike feet, and forward-looking eyes.

rectilinear: Moving in a straight line.

roost: A place where birds settle to rest at night.

ruminant: A mammal that chews cud.

savanna: A grassy plain with few trees.

scrub country: Land covered with brushwood and stunted trees.

stalk: Pursue or approach stealthily.

swamp: An area of low-lying ground where water collects.

talon: A claw belonging to a bird of prey.

troop: A group of animals of a particular kind.

tundra: A vast, flat, treeless Arctic region in which the subsoil is permanently frozen.

vertebrae: Small bones that form the backbone with a hole through which the spinal cord passes.

vole: Small mouselike rodent.

vulnerable: Subject to physical attack or harm.

webbed: The feet of an aquatic animal with the toes connected by a membrane.